I0714038

FlowerSong Press
McAllen, Texas 78501

Copyright © 2021 by KRISTINE ESSER SLENTZ

ISBN 978-1-953447-69-2
Library of Congress Control Number: 2021936872

Published by FlowerSong Press
in the United States of America.
www.fl owersongpress.com

Typeset and design by Chris Cline and KRISTINE ESSER SLENTZ

No part of this book may be reproduced without written permission from the publisher.

All inquiries and permission requests should be addressed to the publisher.

woman, depose

KRISTINE ESSER SLENTZ

"It felt like my story was being erased. So, I
needed to change the narrative… I'm much more
comfortable with honesty than trying to act like
I'm a perfect woman."

— JoJo, UPROXX interview

UNITED ███ DISTRICT █████ OF █████ DIVISION

)
)
)
)
)
)
)
)
)

MOTION

her

sexual ████ violation

judgment asks █████ to find

support

ME: The last thing I want to do is cause more dysfunction. I want to try to eliminate that as much as possible. I know when someone leaves that at some point that is inevitable.

2

Frames

You add lavender to Your bedding.
I lie on the edge looking at You
unfold You notice My thick plastic glasses.
You ask how poor
is My vision. I say bad. I take off
the spectacles, offering them to You.
You shake Your head, no.
You don't want to get a headache looking through My lenses.
I place the frames back on My face
I get up from Your plush mattress.
I finish pulling on the fitted sheet.

fucking poem

down sweating passion
        raise catholicism up
                to meet shattered middles

my vodka-crippled hands
        sliding up addict blades
                i thrust broken nails

permit exhilaration on our creamy
        slaps and coarse-botched curls
                with freshly dipped regret

penetrate long family guilt past
        our other pursed frozen pipes that
                spread over minty mouths

then with a flick
        with my ass aching for fevers
                to sink his substances

into awaiting stepfamily
        the head ghosts forward
                to assist release souls' rapture

preference to push bullets
        shamed by his thick hands
                extend powerful ecstasy

while imprints his angel palms
        holding hard onto my heart cheeks
                bed begin quickly manifesting

forgotten fluids fly over our
        dropping out strength
                frenzied underrated friction

persistent caress of my explosives
        rapid pounding by damned
                ignites townie instinct

finally expelling cult contraband of climax
        all over piss part and my sand dunes
                his electric juice that was a strawberry patch

between intertwined less money intimates
        added now no school waited wanting
                that only enhanced our forbidden

facts stated are not necessarily objectively true

fistful

He states
His palm
is just the
back side
of His
knuckles

movement, gentlewoman

soft ribs appreciate muscles to gape up
observing the ascending white ceiling sunset
screaming in kerosene-colligated colors
like the blood-spotting left on these king linens
a rooster's night has come cackling now
and this shades broadcast is its evidence

like journalists coded inked evidence
read between unchangeable elbows up
can't but to cry over clinching covers now
wishes refuse dark spell would give its sunset
so confinement beneath cellblock linens
with an assorted surprise of gasping colors

not the comfort of an uptown fur coats' colors
or the contentment of a guild pigeon's evidence
instead pinned on push-springs in treated linens
wishing more good legs and eyes dangling up
casting another end life's dreaming sunset
the mattress's heartbeat ghost breathes now

knowing there is no honor quivering now
aware of red costs in our rainbow colors
facing enveloped straightness at year's sunset
kill of touch towering retrospective evidence
climb lower animal breath pending stands up
that's right, for hire washes your stained linens

mine and her justice waters lost our linens
mother's fingers are nightmare wary now
kitchen utterances of mated fear, what's up
dousing includes regret and walking magic colors
fire humans can't smoke wound evidence
the foot drops and will cast his lost sunset

then weeping council's approach to stalk sunset
release cloud-forehead of compound cage linens
no taking sideways walk, slippery-haired evidence
steel heavens of women breaking method now
elasticity of milk grass and rod light colors
permission love and lush view, won't gave up

think room of stopped mega moons time's up
turning forever heat-lamp constellation colors
the sky is sick, me too, it's her body's space now

daddy

placebo daddy
grease hissing tooth
pinkest longing legs

wolf daddy
drool blood over legs
daylong orphan cock

makeshift daddy
boneless legs moan too
long halo sinks spit pills

hacked daddy
pull on cured legs legacy
sweet milk of long desert

Daddy   daily glisten this crotchless princess
your princess   queen
your self-appointed queen

SUBJECT LINE: USAGE NOTIFICATION
ACCOUNT NUMBER * *** 8187**

Dear Mary,

We want to notify you that you have used 100% of your daughter
anytime usage allowance with your family plan for the service date
ending on this Sunday die to religious affiliation.

Generally, should you reach your capacity limit for any payment
cycle, your love and compassion speeds will be significantly reduced.

To view your usage or purchase additional emotional capacity, please
visit the website.

Thank you for being a valued customer.

*Please do remember that the daughter entity retains the right to
end the unconditional contract anytime as well.

4

At*

*seventeen
"you should have known better
he has a kid"

the reply i received
from the first adult
i trusted to tell

"i was raped"

*twenty-five
"she's an adult
she makes her own decisions"

the argument to abandon me
from a false friend

who should've helped

"what happened to me"

the way is born: the way is born: faces the breaking

faces the breaking

from refined grains into panes

through sounds of suffocation

fragments of finger feelings

the way is born:

from refined grains into panes

5

lilly demons, lurking

running sound
had authority to
affect her
Post about dating as a bisexual woman
he "just laughed and said it was interesting."
learned remarks
required to attend a sit-down meeting

It's true.
Pacing back with delicate greed, I submit this heartfelt damage:
I am a demon to you.

The system knelt to us with a distorted masculine scent,
feeling like a screw, we chewed its loops of ravaged mirrors.

Then the exposure of his paws risked torment into back-slide
so that phantom pain trills and heavy vermouth became ritual.

Twitching winged evils will always accrue here on earth
with our grime-covered-blank-faces mimicking each other's sins.

So, we feed drops of pain on to one another's heart bulge,
a cue that all subliminal souls are flagrantly mismanaged.

Those devils are undaunted in subduing us humans.
Every living being is just satan's squirming baggage,
it's true.

I am a demon to you.

my grunts burst into feathers

white candy-striped midnight
gutted throat's snot pockets
down on Franklin Ave's stall
try three to four more pounds
of pearls collide with the face
lockjaw leopard swelling liquid
mirror glances to see rim cock
penny drop of course not bills
druggy desserts backed pain
fingerprint goodness fades like
kneecap puns or gloved meat
laced up orphans enjoy spunk
pulsing swarms enter cemetery
waving eye rolls and dark stars

my chronic caress cries barred

text messages late at night

6

indiana(polis)
after Tim Dlugos's ALLENTOWN

sleeping to
sunshine and
still being
stoned and
trying to
stay virginal before
sundown comes

<u>**EXHIBIT**</u>

HER: It's a lot of unfair in a lot of ways.

45

instructed all inappropriate behavior
brushed off the incident

ME: They were relentless. It just wears on you. I know in the scheme of things they are insignificant but when you have someone coming to you every other day complaining about you and telling whoever they can how terrible you are it wears on you, you know?

limited resources   provided

depose
de
tory
pre
mores
pressing
ing
memorie
come
depress
an
post
ring
decompose
decomposing
sure
posturing
ast
tion
manifest
bering
store
ion
ressing
mposing
associating
co
comp
turns
ning
remember
osing
me
ompos
or
su
composure
turning
morie
ember
remembering
more
memories
pos
compose
sociate
memoring
oir
os
posure
tories
soci
ifest
memory
ate
ber
ating

posture
mor
rem
fest
pro
compost
associate
ne
memor
ture
on
decomp
story
ress
press
stay
depressing
as
so
ess
posing
deposing
i
stories
tes
com
member
soc
oi
asso
pose
if
ass
turn
dis
ories
man
ting
ure
urn
members
disassociate
st
ir
composing
membering
tore
say
past
mem
omp
at
ay
sing
pr
es
deposition

9

HER: It's hard. It feels hateful.

ask me
Ask me how
Ask Me
Ask ME
Ask Me
Ask Me
Ask mE
Ask ME
Ask me
ask Me
ask me
Ask me
ask. ME
ASK ME
ASK ME
ASK ME
ASK ME
ASK ME

called her a "bitch"

In response

10

careful slain

compress air
molecules cold
choke anger
down travel
sustain slush
hit tree
snaps
broken sidewalk
slab across
ground cover
rain

sex: guilty

living cockroaches
transform metropolitan
prized virginity

11

unstilled spirits

clearly bottled
transparent & transparent
see-through
see it through

nothing through
not through
never through
never enough

never done
even when it's done
it's not done
not until you are done

words heard
heard words
words never heard
heard never words
never heard words
words heard never
words never word
word never heards
nevers words word
words never heards
heards nevers word
heards never heard
never word nevers
words words words
heards heards heard
never never nevers
word nevers never
heards ever word
hear ever or
ear eve   **or worsened**

demonstrate

reasonable steps to remedy the harassment

12

ceremonial of spouse

late-night breakfasts waited up
between time to traded chairs
moth-bitten kisses broken cup
to share

hard-pressed counter sweats
and ∞ wishes barreled stare
teething packs silver cigarettes
to share

with living destroyed luck bare
passed long-lasting rib to share

repeat

i haven't been crying so hard that my sinuses feel like
they are about to bleed down to the forearms that were the
only protection that still got punished

repeat   **repeat**

this happens to those who wait, work, and waste though the
tale was always those who kill themselves are committing
murder on their own wet flesh, but with another's fingers

repeat   **repeat**   **repeat**

using kind trickery & knowingly no blessing of permission
permits Him to reach past my twisted elbows to pull for a
kiss on overly covered cunt

repeat   **repeat**   **repeat**   **repeat**

—clearly and directly—

notice sexual harassment

basement sect sacrifices the beyond

ate that bond armor
at dusk filled doctrine fists
by throwing it
up-sided down
look at that shake
on shelves — door-to-door

He was never there
ratted thrones make ice tea
or is she a bitch?
psh — that's right, cowgirl
we'll grab pizza squares
to the next door, drag-on

it was real, wasn't it
was it too loud — or quick
i could never tell
cult, cult, cult
you hated every drop
wrinkling to your walk

when did the Goliaths get in
the night before that picked path
yeah, i said it
bush fire, bush fire, bush fire
hands over explosive book(s)
the wine killed itself again

whisper that shit
cock that face-loaded
then skip dinner to piss in bed
fuck sales, man
virginity cost money to have
only if there is extra icing

hear that — in the back
it's that tick again
howl at the wall, wall
she will hear you — promise
white lace is gross
it means rape — rape

HA — no — no
she loved his gun shot
with shy wrists and gums
fuck harder screamed
died, olive, open cornfield
burn it down to the circle

left-hand hawkeyes sass stars
the sound of gravel haunts me
slippery sleep, even now
trees wave at your shook
armchair gives pins and pens
look, they have no windows

unsee color ties to knee-length skirts
what was taken, who
look around for them — run
downstairs was potato chips and
deep sex couches with sharks
rush home for porridge

did the umbrella teeth suck you
lucky bastards of masks
decades of yellow linens
they cursed the vagina
of premediated apples leaning
dark days are here

sautéed skin looks good on you
ring the buzzer — ring
universe of my university
make it to the mock treasure
smell the menstrual blood from here
beat passion with past pickles

don't worry — they'll escape
horse, horse, horse, horse man
when do I deserve to die
I just wanted to be a cat
He took the pussy
by mouth-of-word

tomorrow their giants arrives
servants are donut holes — but happy
she surfs papercuts — He licks them
everyone blinks every time
downtown hell, of course
shimmer shit like tin washboards

did the sparkler fade dreams too
seems like it, songs
hard candy fought silk flowers yesterday
the pencil sharpener walked out
Tuesdays are the worst
and Thursdays

when did your belly button break
own hand, me down on red
fountain of flakes with touching
tickle to low suffocation scared
right, all of them robbed
eyeballs, meet tongue

14

I Live

I've lived with ghosts, cockroaches, and raccoons
I've lived with calico cats, dirty dogs, and an orange rabbit
I've lived with metropolitan mice, rural rats, and a possum

I've lived with substance shame, sex regret, and family guilt
I've lived with half family, stepfamily, and chosen family
I've lived with parents having hepatitis C, cancer, and depression
I've lived with a boyfriend, husband, and myself

I've lived with translated bibles, botched brochures, and bullets
I've lived with a cult, Catholicism, and paganism
I've lived with broken nails, fevers, and souls
I've lived with virtuous monsters, powerful misfits, and damned
angels

I've lived with gin, vodka, and Vicodin
I've lived with alcoholics, drug addicts, and myself
I've lived with DUIs, IUDs, and EODs

I've lived with migraines, stomach ulcers, and sobriety
I've lived with a rape, break-in, and a shattered kitchen window
I've lived with punches, slaps, and a bite
I've lived with frozen pipes, hearts, and beds

I've lived with abuse, manipulation, and manifestation
I've lived with being fought over, fucked with, and forgotten
I've lived with passion, persistence, and piss
I've lived with devastation, underestimation, and exhilaration

I've lived with ancestors of colonizers, the colonized, and the lost
I've lived with green cards, citizens, and those undocumented
I've lived with sand dunes, bright lights, and suburban flights

I've lived with self-harm, self-awareness, and self-care
I've lived with couples' therapy, group therapy, and medication
I've lived with hyper-sexuality, bisexuality, and prized virginity
I've lived with homeschool, public school, and dropping out

I've lived with beige carpet, linoleum, and pressed-wood walls
I've lived with a broken-down car, station wagon, and pickup truck
I've lived with no money, less money, and sometimes money
I've lived with patches of strawberries, clovers, and rosemary

I've lived I've lived I've lived
I have lived   I have lived   I have lived

I live

15

asses

boys were laughing after
he joked about asses after

he ran out of the room
I was left on a king size bed after

plunging pain still pulsing up my core
he threw me turned over coming down after

pinched my hips tight with one hand
doused my asshole in lube with the other after

drunkenly plopped my drunken self
falling into the room after

taking jello shots, twisting tongues
enough to create catcallers after

i told him i loved him, he said me too
to help prevent further cheating after

i punched him in the ribs when he said he
would do whatever he wanted, me crying after

realizing toxicity delivers more pain than change after
listen, sweet children, you must stop this cycle after

knot running
after Luzene Hill's art installation
"Retracing the Trace"

the run of a yarn
a long pathway
of foggy memories

she is outlined
not in white chalk —
those are leaves

or knots, not
just strings
wrapped to

keep petrified cries
and battle breath
from escaping

pulled so stiff
around her
resilient throat

cannot stop her
signs of struggle
on this earth

that she will tell
in voice, vision,
and vindication

not from him
or your sorrow
but from knots

of passed ancestors
from living elders
and us who have gone now

because she failed to check the retaliation box

**ode to a new
worshipping of
the cunt**

our constructed
gazes meet.

my crown
rests on this
throne while you kneel
serving us
both, best.

now,
spread your teeth
and bare the soft, wet
muscle inside your mouth
that is available
for my pleasure, alone.

my hands tighten
on wooden frames
and yours on
the floor boards.

I allow you to enjoy
the feast I provide
that you came to me
and begged for.

I smile as I feel all
the benefits of glory,
I then move my fingers
to the top of your head
to bless your gifts of lust.

and, you are happy
to accept once you
have finished worshipping
my majesty that gives
life.

I finish with you
and then give a nod
to rise, you come to
your shaking feet and
eyes cast glances
waiting for permission
that I grant upon soft
words and slow gestures.

our constructed
gazes meet,
a means
to our end.

ME: When one stops and another one starts, you know, what do you do?

17

ME: I'm at the point where there's just always so many emotions in my life that I'm starting to just like, I can't right now, you know what I mean? You know, I've had the emotions right now so I'm just not going to right now.

HER: You're numb.

ME: Yeah. Yeah.

My Love Line

He enters my eye line.

His beauty defined by jawlines,
despite our social lines.

Ok, I can't get over our party line.
So, let's skip the bathroom line.

Did I tell you my pickup line?
Did you just do a line?

Left a line for us to trespass
beyond stated lines.

Please, either ride the line or
line me with a stronger one.

Well, my credit line has brought
him — a line of ignorance.

He enters my sidelines.

harassment that she "loved"

Final judgment

enter accordingly

18

<u>EXHIBIT</u>

ME: I feel like there was a few people pushing.

HER: Maybe it's because I felt pushed. I don't know.

ME: It's ok. We'll figure it out.

HER: Think about what you need.

"Yeah, bitch, I'm still here!"
    — JoJo, UPROXX interview

Photo Credit - Victor Giganti

Originally, from northwest Indiana and the Chicagoland area, KRISTINE is a Purdue University alum who double majored in English Literature and Creative Writing. Recently, she earned her MFA in Creative Writing (poetry) from City College of New York where she currently is an Adjunct Assistant Professor. KRISTINE was a finalist for the 2020-21 Glass Poetry Chapbook Contest and Spring 2020 Flash Fiction Contest for F(r)iction. Additionally, she was Pushcart Prize nominated, awarded the 2020-21 Rifkind Fellowship and CCNY Teacher-Writer Award, and currently is completing a writing residency with Poets Afloat.

Thank You

Chi Sherman — Your presence on this planet is a blessing, particularly to me. You are the first and last eyes on basically all of my writing and oftentimes the tragedies that proceed them. Thank you for your kindness, brilliance, and friendship.

Constantine Jones — You're the sweetest. The energy in which you not only give your feedback but live life is enchanting and powerful. So, so much gratitude to you!

Hannah Cohen — I'm so honored that you agreed to read over such an early draft of this manuscript. Not only that, you encouraged me in such a lovely way. Thank you!

Joanna Valente — Your work is so inspiring. I appreciate your sharp editorial eyes on this manuscript during its drafting journey. I hope to keep experiencing both of these talents of yours endlessly!

Nicole Sealey — Your dedication to your students and the community is unwavering. Thank you for all your insights while I was in the CCNY MFA program. Your workshops were truly a bonding experience.

Cynthia Cruz — Your notes and guidance during my time in the CCNY MFA program were so pivotal in the development of this work. I'm in much gratitude to you.

Helene Fisher — I knew right when we started the MFA program together we were going to be cool. Helene, thank you for always seeing my work. Not to mention, you're a fantastic friend and creator.

Leah Beatty — Your support is unlike anything I've experienced and if it wasn't for it I'm not sure how far I would be in my writing/ personal journey. Thank you, for everything.

Michelle Valladares — You're the best. That's it. You're simply amazing and I wish everyone could take a workshop with you.

Laura Hinton — Your classes and mentorship came at such an important time in my life and this collection. Your knowledge and push truly made me a better writer.

Emily Kuhn — Thank you for your support and openness, always. You're the greatest, most lovable accountant ever. Seriously.

Melinda Worst — You're my family. I'm so grateful to have you in my life — especially while I was working through so many of the topics discussed in this book. Mel, you're the princess!

Jaray Hunt — You're a spectacular human who writes spectacular words. Thank you for forever impacting my life and work.

Carly Kincannon — Thank you for always holding space for me.

Megan Brown — Your reassurance during some of the darker moments of my life really helped comfort me and put things into perspective. Your badassness is the shit of legend. Thank you for that.

Sonja Killebrew — Your joy lights up everything, including this book. Your encouragement moved the many foothills that surrounded this collection and beyond.

Matt Gahler — How many tears (or should I say fears) of mine have you seen? Your kindness, wit, and creative ability is cherished.

Jack Trottier — You helped keep me alive all these years.

Lincoln Slentz — To the man I am married to, Pizza. Heart.

Previously Published Poems

"frames"
forthcoming *Pink Plastic House*

"fucking poem"
Queen Mob's Tea House

"fistful"
forthcoming *Pvssy Magic Magazine*

"movement, gentlewoman"
Pvssy Magic Magazine &
America's Emerging Poets 2018: NY & NJ

"daddy"
Kissing Dynamite Punk Anthology

"subject line"
Flying Island Journal & *Barren Magazine*

"At*"
Rag Queen Periodical

"faces breaking"
Juke Joint Magazine

"lilly demons, lurking"
Bold City Literary Magazine

"feathers"
Glass Poetry

"Indiana(polis)"
Rose Quartz Magazine

"ask me, how to"
Moonchild Magazine

"careful slain"
Juke Joint Magazine

"sex: guilty"
Queen Mob's Tea House

"unstilled spirits"
NY's Best Emerging Poets 2019: Anthology

"ceremonial of spouse"
Queen Mob's Tea House

"repeat" poem
Philosophical Idiot

"basement sect sacrifices of the beyond"
Crab Fat Magazine

"asses"
Rose Quartz Magazine

"knot running"
RECLAIM Anthology

"ode to a new worshipping of the cunt"
Pvssy Magic Magazine

"My Love Line"
Pvssy Magic Magazine

"I Live"
Pvssy Magic Magazine

www.ingramcontent.com/pod-product-compliance
Lightning Source LLC
Chambersburg PA
CBHW080726210726
48292CB00016B/2919